Dr. Death

Life of Serial Killer Michael Swango

Jack Smith

Disclaimer and Terms of Use

Effort has been made to ensure that the information in this book is accurate and complete. However, the author and the publisher do not warrant the accuracy of the information, text, and graphics contained within the book due to the rapidly changing nature of science, research, known and unknown facts, and internet. The author and the publisher do not hold any responsibility for errors, omissions, or contrary interpretation of the subject matter herein. This book is presented solely for motivational and informational purposes only.

Warning

Throughout the book there are some descriptions of murders and crime scenes that some people might find disturbing.

Note

Words in italic are quoted words from verbatim and have been reproduced as is, including any grammatical errors and misspells.

ISBN: 978-1983684753

Printed in the United States

MAPLEWOOD
– PUBLISHING –

Contents

Contents

The Exception to the Rule

Joseph Michael Swango was born on October 21, 1954, the same year that Senator Joseph McCarthy was censured, ending the long reign of political terror that McCarthy had instigated against perceived enemies of the state. This other Joseph coming into this slightly thawing Cold War world wouldn't get too much into politics as he grew older, but he would one day conduct his own personal reign of terror that would leave at least 60 people dead. Just looking at the diabolical end results of Michael Swango's life begs the oft-asked question: Were there any warning signs?

If you are attempting to look for the exact formula that created this killer, you certainly won't find it in the town where he was raised. Michael Swango grew up in the idyllic confines of Quincy, Illinois, a quaint piece of Mid-America that doesn't exactly present itself as a monster factory. It's just one of many nondescript, safely middle-class towns in the American heartland. Michael was the middle of three children born to John and Muriel Swango. His mother Muriel tried to create a nice home for her children, and by all accounts she was a loving parent.

However, the Swango kids would later recall a few odd things about their childhood, such as the fact that their mother never seemed to want to invest in wrapping paper for Christmas presents. She would simply put their gifts in brown paper bags, staple them shut, and shove them under the tree. But no matter how unconventional that may be, would the fact that Swango's mom brown paper bagged Christmas make him a serial killer? Probably not; it didn't make his siblings into any such thing. And odd little idiosyncrasies aside, Muriel did at least try to create a loving home for her kids. That wasn't always easy, since she was often left by herself to do it.

Her husband, John, was rarely ever home. Michael Swango's father was a very busy man, a real mover and shaker in the United States military who served as a career officer all throughout the exceedingly unpopular Vietnam War. Like many soldiers of that era, Michael's dad was deeply affected by the reception he was given upon his return to the States. The war itself was bad enough, but that was to be expected; but John Swango found that how he was treated and perceived by his fellow citizens was even worse.

While the soldiers of World War Two and the Korean War were perceived as heroes and given ticker-tape parades, John Swango and the men he led in Vietnam were less than universally acclaimed. Those who believed what they heard on the evening news about American GIs burning down villages and brutalizing innocent civilians could not see these men as heroes who had sacrificed everything for their country. They were treated with suspicion at worst, and pity at best. Facing such psychological pressure in the early 1970s—a time before PTSD was a household word, a time in which such dysfunction was often incomprehensible to the public—Michael's father began to drown his demons in alcohol.

He sunk into an impenetrable void of depression, and as a result young Michael's family soon broke apart in divorce. Michael's father was almost completely out of his life after this, and Michael became even more dependent on his mother, to a degree that some described as "clingy." As Michael progressed through adolescence, it seemed that he wanted to impress

Muriel and win her approval more than anything else—and he succeeded admirably.

He became an accomplished musician, learning to play the piano and playing the clarinet in the school band. He managed to attain the position of first chair, and eventually became so good that the band teacher, who also played in a professional symphony orchestra, had him take part in their seasonal tour while he was still a senior in high school.

Nor was music the only area in which Michael excelled. He made A's and B's throughout his high school career, and he became the valedictorian of his graduating class in 1972. Far from the stereotype of an isolated loser who grows up to commit heinous crimes, Michael was a well-adjusted and really popular kid. He seemed to get along well with just about everyone, and no problems with classmates or teachers were ever reported. Due to his popularity and accomplishments both academic and extracurricular, Michael Swango was even elected class president.

The story so far doesn't exactly seem to reflect the origins of a misanthrope and sociopath, does it? No, Michael Swango's youth doesn't fit the profile of such highly depraved characters—but of course, there is always an exception to every rule.

4

Pursuing Excellence

Shortly after his high school graduation, Swango began attending Millikin University in Decatur, Illinois, just a three-hour drive from his hometown of Quincy. With Swango's grades and SAT scores he could have attended school just about anywhere, but it seems in these early years he wanted to stay close to home. At Millikin, a small liberal arts college, Swango excelled well above and beyond his peers, with his GPA reaching the crystalized perfection of a 4.0. But on a personal level, the formerly positive and chipper Michael Swango began to have his ups and downs.

His world changed somewhere around his sophomore year in college and a messy breakup with his first serious girlfriend. This breakup seems to have hit Swango particularly hard and left a lasting psychological impact on him. Friends say that after the breakup he started to act and dress differently. Previously he had dressed in conservative khakis and polo shirts; now he began to wear all-out military attire. His friends knew that he came from a military family, but Swango wasn't in the military at the time, so they didn't quite know what to make of it.

Remember that Swango was doing this right at the height of the Vietnam War, when many of his peers were burning draft cards and otherwise attempting to stay as far away from the military as possible. For him to sport such pro-military attire was really pretty bizarre in the early 1970s. And then Swango took things a step further and joined the military himself. In a seemingly random, spur-of-the-moment decision, he abruptly left Millikin

University after his sophomore year, enlisted with the Marines, and went to basic training for the summer. Was he trying to follow in his father's footsteps?

Perhaps, but at this point he wasn't even in contact with his dad. If he was trying to impress or gain his father's approval, he had no way of even letting him know about it. Nevertheless, Swango seemed to excel in the military; he even obtained the special rank of "sharpshooter" for his prowess with a rifle. Not a lot is known about Swango's service, but according to the public record he made the rounds. He entered into training at the base in St. Louis and was eventually transferred to Camp Lejeune in North Carolina, where he was ultimately given an honorable discharge in 1976.

Swango was not only honorably discharged, he also received a number of medals, including distinctions such as the Meritorious Mast and the Defense Service Medal. Swango never went to war, and his reasons for leaving the service are as unclear as his reasons for enlisting in the first place. But leave it he did, stepping away from active duty in the Marines to pick up his academic career where he had left it behind. He enrolled as a full-time student at Quincy University in his hometown of Quincy, Illinois—and immediately began to stand out like a sore thumb due to his military mannerisms and attire.

It was later discovered that Swango had greatly embellished his military record on his application to Quincy. Despite never having seen combat, he claimed to have received the Bronze Star and a Purple Heart for his service, which were both outright lies. But regardless of the deception, he was once again an ideal student, obtaining a GPA of 3.89, well above most of his classmates. He double majored in biology and chemistry and expressed an interest in attending medical school, and to most he seemed to be on the fast track to doing so.

But in stark contrast to his earlier years, Swango was becoming quite isolated during his time at Quincy University. His only real extracurricular activity was spending late nights in the science lab to conduct chemistry research and experiments. This fascination with chemistry prefigured later years when he was accused of putting together lethal chemical compounds with which to poison his patients. But even more shockingly telling in retrospect was Swango's senior thesis, which discussed the assassination of Georgi Markov.

Markov was a Bulgarian writer and dissident who was exiled in Great Britain. He worked on foreign affairs for the BBC, and was a vocal critic of Communism in general and Bulgaria in particular. It is believed that he was killed by a Soviet-backed Bulgarian agent in London. Georgi was waiting at a bus stop to catch a ride to the BBC station when he felt a sharp pain in his leg. He turned to see a man next to him fumbling with an umbrella. The man simply muttered, "Sorry," and went on his way.

Georgi assumed that this "Umbrella Man" (as the mysterious figure was later called) had simply bumped into him, but when he arrived at the BBC station to begin his shift, it became clear that there was something more to this seemingly random incident. Georgi soon became deathly ill and had to be rushed to the hospital. He would die just a few days later from what was later determined to be a lethal dose of ricin that had been injected into his leg.

This lethal toxin was precisely the kind of chemical that Swango had been experimenting with so intently at the science lab at Quincy, and it would come to prominence in his later crimes as well. Swango graduated from Quincy University in 1979 with an award from the American Chemical Society for academic excellence. If only they knew that Michael Swango's "excellence" would one day be used for murder!

8

Some Serious Medicine

Swango was accepted into the Southern Illinois University (SIU) School of Medicine that same year and was already attending classes by the fall. The sprawling campus of SIU is situated in the Illinois state capital of Springfield, with further campuses in Edwardsville and Carbondale. Here, Swango once again immersed himself in his studies, and once again he took an incredible amount of interest in courses on pharmacology, toxicology, and pathology. Any course that dealt with chemistry, drugs, disease, and lethal toxins was always on Swango's short list while at SIU.

Swango made it a point to live a rigid lifestyle at SIU. His classmates were often amused—if not slightly disturbed—to find him doing pushups and other military-style exercises outside on campus grounds. He also continued to wear military attire, which continued to set him apart from his more stylish peers. At med school, his study habits also set him apart.

Notes were strictly forbidden during test time, but Swango had developed a way around this. He would begin taking a test and then make an excuse to go out into the hallway and cram his notes on the fly before coming back in to answer the questions. This underhanded method seemed to work for him, and as he aced test after test with this strategy, some of his classmates took notice and began to copy his system. This little loophole for accessing notes eventually became so epidemic that teachers began to call it "Swangoing" and specifically told their students before a test, "There will be no Swangoing."

The next thing that Swango would become famous for during his tenure at SIU was his dissection method. Dissecting a corpse is a rite of passage for all med students, but when the turn came for Swango to dissect a cadaver, the results were so gruesome that the rest of his classmates would never forget it. Instead of a body with clean incisions and organs neatly removed, the corpse was a mangled mess of formaldehyde-preserved flesh. Classmates said it looked like Swango had done his dissecting with a chainsaw rather than a scalpel. It was actually so bad that even Swango had to admit that there was no way he could continue with his handiwork, so when it came time for him to present his findings to the class, he had to rely on pictures from his textbook rather than the desecrated corpse right in front of him.

But despite these oddities, Swango was able to persevere. By his final year of med school, he had chosen neurosurgery as his specialty and was given real-world work in the hospital under residency staff. Most had a distinct disdain for Swango, but he did gain the admiration of one of the neurosurgeons, a man named Dr. Lyle Wacaser. Where others saw bizarre eccentricity, Dr. Wacaser saw a hard-working genius. To most faculty, though, Swango's hard work and dedication to the field seemed to be paying off in a negative way. They began to notice that more patients than usual expired when Swango was administering treatment.

Some of the other med students, perhaps recalling Swango's military background, then crafted what they felt was a fitting nickname for the strange medical intern. They began calling him "Double-O Swango" in reference to the James Bond movies in which "OO" agents were licensed to kill. This was predominantly just the morbid humor of med students and faculty who spent many late nights together and often witnessed tragic events. They never really believed what they were saying; for them it was just a joke. The only trouble was that Michael Swango wasn't laughing. And soon he would show them all just how serious he was.

Swango Gets His License

Michael Swango was in his last year of med school when he received word that his father had passed away. It was shortly after New Year's, in January of 1982, that Muriel placed the phone call that would send her son back to Quincy. At his father's funeral, everyone Swango met was impressed with how far he had come. They saw an ambitious, handsome young man speaking of his life on the fast track to being a neurosurgeon and felt that Swango was hands down the star of the entire family.

But his illustrious future career in medicine was not quite as assured as the relatives at his dad's funeral believed. In fact, in his last month of med school, he was nearly kicked out altogether. It was Swango's cavalier attitude and cocky self-assurance that led to his near dismissal. He had been finishing up one of his last requirements, a mandatory observational course in OB/GYN at the hospital, when it was revealed that he had been fudging all of his H & P (History and Physical) reports. He had been observed going into patients' rooms for less than ten minutes and then coming back with full-length reports that normally took 30 to 45 minutes to complete.

Suspecting something wasn't right, doctors investigated Swango's H & P reports and discovered that they had indeed been completely fabricated. This alone was enough grounds to have Swango expelled, but luck would intervene on his behalf. When a hearing was held to determine what to do with him, there was one dissenting vote in his favor. Without a unanimous decision to dismiss him, he was allowed to go forward and finish med school. Amazingly, even with such a poor track record at SUI, Swango was able to gain a spot for himself at Ohio State University Medical Center in 1983 after sending out a flurry of applications all over the Midwest.

Swango was able to beat out 60 other applicants for this residency, primarily because of how convincing he was in his personal interview. Swango, as odd as some of his mannerisms could be, was usually able to leave a good impression. He always seemed to know just the right things to say, and apparently that was enough to convince the gatekeepers at the Ohio Medical Center to give him a chance. He signed an agreement that would grant him a residency in neurosurgery after a 12-month internship in general surgery starting on the 1st of July, 1983.

Not long after his arrival, many patients under his care began to become gravely ill, and some died. Nursing staff in Rhodes Hall, where Swango was assigned, began to take note of the unusually high amount of "Code Blues" that occurred while he was present. One of these Code Blues was a patient named Ruth Barrick. Ms. Barrick had checked into the hospital on January 17th for head trauma resulting from a fall.

In the immediate aftermath of the fall she had suffered from a fairly serious cerebral hematoma. However, she was quickly stabilized upon arriving at the medical center, and was now in fair condition, seeming to improve every day. Her progress dramatically reversed itself on January 31st, however, after an impromptu bedside visit by Doctor Swango. According to one of the attending nurses that morning, a woman named Deborah Kennedy, she had given Ruth Barrick her breakfast meal, and found her in good health, communicative, and following instructions well.

It was right in the middle of her checkup with Ruth, around 9:45 in the morning, that Swango appeared and informed the nurse that he needed to check on the patient. Deborah then left the room, allowing Swango space for whatever procedures he needed to carry out. Less than twenty minutes later, she returned to find that her previously healthy patient had turned blue and was barely breathing. The nurse immediately called out a Code Blue, and as medical personnel rushed onto the scene, Swango was one of the first to respond.

With a group effort, the team was able to revive the ailing patient. She was then stabilized and sent to the ICU for recovery. Ruth was once again doing very well when on February 6th a nurse named Anne Ritchie happened to notice that one of her IVs seemed to be malfunctioning. She called for a doctor to come down to help with the equipment, and none other than Swango arrived. The nurse then excused herself and allowed Swango to get to work.

Swango drew the curtains around Ruth's bed shut, obscuring his handiwork, but the Nurse Ritchie periodically peeked in to see if she could be of assistance. At one point she witnessed Swango working on the IV with several unknown syringes. She asked if he needed help, but he was adamant that he didn't, so she stayed out of his way after that. Several more minutes passed before she finally saw Swango leave the patient's room. The nurse then came in to check on the patient and was horrified to find her gasping for air immediately before going into complete cardiac arrest.

Just like Nurse Kennedy before her, Nurse Ritchie frantically called out a Code Blue. This time, however, Swango had stuck around to see the results of his handiwork. He came right back around the corner to witness the frazzled nurse attempting to give the dying patient CPR. Instead of trying to be a hero and lending his help, he just stepped back and cavalierly criticized the nurse's prowess with cardiopulmonary resuscitation.

As he watched her put her mouth on the old woman's in a desperate attempt to breathe life back into her, Swango cruelly remarked, "That is so disgusting." In complete bewilderment at what she was experiencing, the nurse looked away from her dying patient to see Swango staring at her with a satisfied smirk on his face. In disgusted outrage, she screamed at him, "You jerk!" Shortly after this confrontation, the rest of the ER team arrived to try their hand at resuscitation, and Swango slipped away in the chaos.

Unfortunately for Ruth Barrick, she would not survive the swirling medical mayhem Swango had created at her expense. She was pronounced dead a few hours later. The official cause of death was listed as "cardiopulmonary arrest due to cerebrovascular accident." But the two nurses who had personally cared for the patient during her stay at the hospital weren't so sure that what they had witnessed was an accident. They weren't entirely sure what to make of her death, but whatever had happened, they knew that Swango was somehow at fault.

As of yet, no one wanted to consider the possibility that Dr. Swango was purposelessly harming patients. There was, however, some gossip that—perhaps through gross negligence or flat-out incompetence—he was adversely affecting those entrusted to his care.

This suspicion only increased when the head of the nursing staff, Amy Moore, witnessed Swango refusing to administer immediate respiratory aid to a patient who was having obvious difficulty in breathing. Instead, Swango was belligerently insisting that the patient needed to have her heart monitored. The patient's heart was fine, however; it was just her breathing that needed immediate attention. The head nurse actually had to physically intervene, separating Swango from the patient in order to deliver the life-saving treatment she needed for her lungs.

14

Complaints regarding Swango's odd protocol with patients began to pile up—so many that the hospital was forced to conduct an internal investigation. But since they could not find any direct evidence of wrongdoing, all the investigation accomplished was to officially clear him.

Once he had been cleared, Swango was quietly moved to another section of the hospital, away from the complaining patients and coworkers. The hospital administration hoped that this simple measure might solve the problem, and if that problem had in fact been a matter of misunderstandings and personality conflicts with the staff of Rhodes Hall, it might well have done the trick. But not long after Swango was moved to another wing of the hospital, patients mysteriously began to die there as well.

And soon it was not only patients who were becoming mysteriously ill. Soon, Swango's own troublesome coworkers would suffer from a mysterious illness as well. In one incident, Swango generously offered to buy lunch and came back with a bunch of Kentucky Fried Chicken for his coworkers. The only trouble was that this chicken was laced with poison. As soon as they started eating the food, everyone became violently ill, throwing up and developing dangerously high fevers. Swango, meanwhile, was munching on his own choice pieces of chicken and not having any problem whatsoever.

Even with all of these strange occurrences, there was still no real proof of any wrongdoing on Swango's part. But in light of all the anecdotal claims and rumors surrounding this troubled resident, Ohio Medical Center decided not to bring Swango back to finish his residency. They just wanted to put this unsettling chapter behind them, as quietly as they could. This didn't stop Swango from getting his medical license, however, and the med student who had once been derided as "Double-O Swango, license to kill" now had an official license to practice medicine.

Swango's New Job

Swango received his medical license in September of 1984. After obtaining this prize, he moved back to Quincy to find work. He initially lied to his family about why he had left what had been promising opportunities in Ohio. Swango claimed it was just a matter of his own personal preference; he hadn't been able to get along with the medical staff there, so he had chosen not to return. He conveniently omitted the fact that they had declined to *let* him return. In Quincy, Swango found a new job—even though it was a significant demotion—working as an EMT for an ambulance company based out of a local medical facility called Blessing Hospital.

This job was a 24-hour, round-the-clock kind of gig in which the EMTs were constantly on call. Swango greatly enjoyed the thrill and excitement of suddenly being rushed to the scene of an emergency—a scene that often included horrific trauma and severely wounded victims. And while enthusiasm for emergency rescues is a desirable trait for an EMT, his coworkers soon took notice that Swango was just a little bit too enthusiastic about his job. Mark Krzystofczyk, a fellow SIU graduate who worked with Swango during this stint as an EMT, was particularly disturbed by the unbridled enthusiasm that Swango exhibited when they happened upon a fatality.

The sight of a dead body was bizarrely exhilarating for Swango. He even said as much to Krzystofczyk after one of these deadly run-ins, asking him, "Wasn't that great?" Swango made similarly unsettling idle comments to other colleagues from time to time as

17

they rode in the back of the ambulance. He also produced some startling visual material that caused even more unease. He called it his scrapbook, and it was filled with collections that he had made over the years of newspaper clippings and photos of natural disasters, crime scenes, traffic accidents, and various other forms of gory death and destruction.

Sharing these images with his coworkers during their downtime, Swango discussed his fascination with these events openly and at great length. Working as an EMT puts people on the front lines of disaster on a daily basis and is known to create thick skins and dark humor. But Swango's macabre behavior was too much for even these hardened emergency personnel to stomach. Most of his coworkers were sincerely creeped out, but others just chalked up Swango's antics to eccentricity and that same trademark dark humor that they all displayed—if not with quite as much gusto as Swango did.

Besides his obsession with death and destruction, the other thing that his coworkers truly marveled at when it came to Swango was his seemingly endless energy. During this period in his life he appeared to be going on next to no sleep on a routine basis. While he worked in Quincy he still had a girlfriend back in Columbus, Ohio, a nurse named Rita Dumas whom he had met during his residency at OSU, and it wasn't uncommon for him to work a long shift, drive to Columbus to see her, drive back, sleep for just 30 minutes in a break room, and then begin another long shift. The man seemed naturally manic and full of energetic enthusiasm whether he slept or not. Even when his colleagues were zoning out and falling asleep on the job, he was absolutely wired.

In his mania, he often sought to please his colleagues in any way he could. On September 14th, that avid enthusiasm seemed to manifest itself in a box of donuts that Swango laid out in the lounge that the EMTs frequented. Swango happily announced to his comrades, "I got you guys a bunch of doughnuts." His tired and hungry coworkers appreciated the gesture, but there was only one problem: the donuts were poisoned. About 30 minutes after Swango's colleagues consumed the donuts, they all became violently ill, vomiting uncontrollably and becoming horribly sick. Every single one of these emergency first responders had to go to their own emergency room for treatment.

It was suspected that the donuts were responsible, but suspicion did not immediately fall on Swango. Instead, authorities looked into the conditions at the donut shop. This led to an official County Health Department report detailing suspicions of negligence on the part of the vendor. However, the owner of the bakery was adamant that his shop had had no part in compromising the food, and after a thorough inspection of his facility, no indication of food poisoning (either deliberate or accidental) could be found.

Investigators still failed to point the finger at Swango, though; they decided that the donuts must have been contaminated with some unknown stomach virus, causing everyone to get sick. After getting away with his donut contamination, Swango became even more prolific with the poisoning of his coworkers. He poisoned soft drinks on several separate occasions before handing them off to colleagues. He even poisoned a whole pitcher of tea in the break room. Swango was soon universally suspected of tampering with his coworkers' food and beverages, but the smoking gun didn't come until he rushed off on ambulance duty and left an open duffel bag behind.

Coworkers discovered that this duffel bag had containers of ant poison inside of it. They theorized that Swango had caused the periodic sickness that had ravaged their ranks by slipping doses of this ant poison into their food and drinks. Samples from the spiked tea were then sent off to a forensics lab, and they were found to contain a direct match for the ant poison in Swango's duffel bag. On October 26, 1984, Swango was arrested and charged with aggravated battery by way of poison.

With Swango in custody, police conducted a search of his apartment and found what could only be described as a kind of chemical laboratory filled with several canisters of toxins and drugs that Swango had apparently been experimenting with. There were vials of ricin, arsenic, and other lethal materials strewn all over the apartment, as well as a small cache of firearms including a shotgun and several handguns. He also had some strange reading materials, such as a thick volume on his coffee table entitled *The Book of Ceremonial Magic*, *The Modern Witch's Spell Book*, and even a copy of the mythical (and mostly fabricated) *Necronomicon*.

In the words of Swango's coworkers, "he was a weird guy." But no one had expected him to have such a bizarre interest in the occult. The well-worn pages of these books, however—along with several pieces of notebook paper with handwritten "spells" on them—seemed to indicate much more than a passing fancy with these dark arts. Just who was Michael Swango, anyway? A doctor? A mad scientist? A mass murderer? An aspiring magician? The deeper anyone delved into his strange and twisted life, the more diabolically mind boggling it all became.

It All Comes Crashing Down

Michael Swango's trial for aggravated battery kicked off on April 22, 1985, with Swango's plea of Not Guilty. His attorney already knew him on a personal level; in fact, his legal counsel was his former high school history teacher. Daniel Cook, not too much older than Swango himself, had returned to school and received his law degree in the years after Swango had left Quincy, and he was eager to defend someone he viewed as "one of his best students."

Following Cook's advice, Swango chose to waive his right to a jury trial and leave his fate in the hands of just one person: trial judge Dennis Cashman. Swango had a host of supportive figures on display in the courtroom, with his mother, brothers, and girlfriend all present. But nearly all of his coworkers at the ambulance company showed up as well. These men all testified against Swango, each offering up his own unique perspective on his character and the likelihood that he had indeed poisoned his colleagues.

These eyewitnesses related account after account of just how obsessed Swango was with violence and death. One of his coworkers even recalled an incident in which Swango had made the offhand remark during a shift that he felt it would "be nice to walk into the Emergency Room and start blowing people away." But of course, as damning as some of these remarks might seem, you cannot convict someone for words alone, and Swango's defense attorney was quick to point this out.

Basically admitting that Swango may have had some odd proclivities, Daniel Cook stated that a verdict of guilt "cannot be based upon guesses, hunches, and baseless opinions." In other words, the defense allowed that Swango might very well be an extremely odd guy, but that didn't make him a poisoner. In order to prove he was capable of that, the prosecution would have to establish much more solid evidence than mere anecdotal recollections from late night banter in and around Blessing Hospital's Emergency Room. In order to get a conviction, they had to connect Swango directly to the crime of poisoning itself.

The prosecution sought to do this through the police reports detailing the stockpiled chemicals found in Swango's apartment, and in particular the ant poison that matched the poison found in the tainted tea from the ER's break room. But the defense was ready for this and brought in their own expert witness, a local exterminator named Kevin O'Donnell. O'Donnell had done his own personal investigation of Swango's apartment and reported that he had discovered many "reddish-type" ants infesting the defendant's living quarters.

According to the defense, this proved that the only reason that Swango had such a large amount of ant poison was that he had an equally large number of ants infesting his apartment. But this appeal to the seemingly common-sense assumption that ant poison was used for ants rather than poisoning coworkers fell flat during cross examination. Under oath, O'Donnell had to admit one peculiar fact about Swango's ant infestation: The ants in his apartment were not normally found in the Midwest; they were more likely natives of Florida.

The prosecution was then quick to point out that Swango's mother had recently moved to a part of Florida that was literally crawling with this type of ants—and coincidentally enough, Swango had recently visited his mother's home in Florida. You could imagine that the ants might have hitched a ride with him on his trip back, but the prosecution asserted that Swango had deliberately brought them to Quincy to build a cover story as to why he had ant poison. Of course, if this was the case, one might wonder why he hadn't just gathered local Midwestern ants to infest his apartment. Why go to all the trouble of bringing ants across state lines?

But any rate, this was the prosecution's stance on the matter, and they were sticking to it. And with all voices and opinions aired out for Judge Cashman's consumption, the entire debate was put to rest on May 2nd. Judge Cashman came back the next day with his verdict. Many in the courtroom were shocked when they heard the words, "On count 1, aggravated battery, I find the defendant Michael Swango not guilty." There was an audible gasp among his former coworkers, and there was suddenly a very real fear that Swango had beat the system and would walk out a free man.

The judge wasn't finished yet, however; he had only read his verdict on one of the seven counts of battery that Swango was facing. And for the remaining six counts, Judge Cashman issued a resounding "guilty as charged." Swango didn't have much of a reaction to the verdict; he simply covered his face with one hand in a muted display of shock. His girlfriend, Rita Dumas, had the most poignant reaction in the courtroom, breaking into heart-wrenching sobs for the man she had thought she was going to spend the rest of her life with.

Swango was then seen trying to hand her a Styrofoam cup, and to add even more drama to what was already a circus, a nearby police officer, fearing that Swango was passing her some sort of poisoned beverage, slapped the cup right out of Swango's hands, causing it to fall to the ground. But this cup didn't hold any coffee, tea, or soda, poisoned or otherwise—it just had a piece of paper inside of it, a piece of paper with the words scrawled in Swango's own handwriting, "I love you, Dumas. Hang in there." Graphologists trained to judge handwriting could spend hours determining whether Swango was sincere—and perhaps pondering why he would refer to his girlfriend by her last name in a love letter!

He wrote "I love you, Dumas." Who really calls his beloved by her last name? Some have even remarked that his scrawled handwriting almost made it look like he wrote "I love you, Dumbass," as if it were one last sick joke to fulfill Swango's sadistic urge to play upon the emotions of the young woman who was indeed desperately in love with him. But we can leave all of this petty speculation to the courtroom junkies and amateur criminal psychologists, because there was one person in that courtroom who could interpret Swango's motives better than anyone else: his mother. And her mind was already made up.

As Swango and Cook huddled outside the courtroom to discuss the possibility of an appeal, Swango's mother and brothers stood in attendance. Swango still insisted he was innocent of all charges and requested Muriel to help him pay the cost of his appeal. Muriel was resolute, however, and with arms crossed, looking right at her convicted son, she shook her head and responded, "I don't have the money". She then looked away and added with certainty, "Anyway, I was there. I know you're guilty. The evidence showed you were guilty."

Just one week later, Muriel would second this opinion about her son to the judge who had convicted him. She had called and scheduled a meeting with the judge shortly after the verdict was rendered. During this meeting she unequivocally stated, "I understand why you reached the decision you did, and I have no quarrel with the verdict." But then, in a sad attempt to rationalize her son's actions, she informed Judge Cashman that her son was "a very troubled young man." She went on to explain that he had become very unsettled after she and her husband had divorced, and had been especially affected by the disconnect that his father seemed to have after his return from service in Vietnam.

She also highlighted Swango's own military service as a factor that had led to his personality change. Although he had avoided combat, Swango had changed considerably when he returned from the Marine Corps, and his mother claimed that he had exhibited symptoms that today might be described as PTSD. She stated that he was easily agitated and seemed to never sleep, as if the threat of the nightmares emerging from the darkness of his troubled psyche was enough to enough to keep him awake at all hours of the day and night.

Muriel may have hoped that these insights into her son's frame of mind would cause the judge to extend some leniency on his behalf. But if this was the case, it had hopelessly backfired, because when the judge read out the sentence that he intended to hand down to Michael Swango, it carried the maximum allotment for the charges leveled against him. On August 23, 1985, Swango was given a sentence of five years in prison.

Some Kind of Nut

After serving only two years of his five-year sentence, Michael Swango was granted supervised release from the Illinois prison system on August 21, 1987, with the stipulation that he would be actively monitored on probation for another 12 months. Swango's most loyal subject upon his release was his girlfriend Rita Dumas, who was there to welcome him back with open arms. In the meantime, Rita had come up with a cleverly concocted story to explain away her beloved boyfriend's conviction. She told anyone who would listen that there was a conspiracy afoot: Swango had actually been framed by the then District Coroner, Wayne Johnson, because Swango had been applying for his job.

Rita was convinced that out of fear of losing his position to the "more skilled" Swango, Johnson had engineered to have Swango prosecuted. These wild assertions perhaps tell us more about Rita's character than anything else. Some have said that if she could believe these outrageous claims, she could probably believe anything. Upon his release, Swango and Rita moved to Virginia, where Swango tried his luck with the Virginia state licensing board, applying to have his medical license renewed there. But the board in Virginia did their homework and ultimately refused his request, citing the numerous red flags that had surfaced around his previous conviction.

Unable to find employment in a hospital, Swango cut his losses and got a job as a counselor at a career development center. But it wasn't long after he began work for this facility that his colleagues began to come down with mysterious illnesses. Here too, his colleagues were alarmed when they saw Swango perusing his scrapbook of death and destruction in the break room and other periods of downtime. But the last straw came when it was revealed that Swango had converted a basement room of the center into his own personal living space. With increasing pressure on him to leave, Swango parted company with the career center in May of 1989.

Shortly after his departure, one of his erstwhile colleagues tipped off the local police department about Swango's strange activities and the spate of unexplained illness that had plagued the career center. The ensuing investigation followed Swango back to Ohio, where Virginia police sought to collaborate with their counterparts in that state in order to find some reason to charge Swango. All of this digging into Swango's activities attracted the attention of the local news media, and a story surfaced in the *Columbus Dispatch* that Swango was under investigation once again.

Nothing resulted from this investigation, but the pressure was enough to prompt Swango to change his name. On January 18, 1990, he had his name officially changed from Joseph Michael Swango to David Jackson Adams. In the meantime, he had also finally married his longtime girlfriend Rita Dumas, on July 8, 1989. With a name change and a new wife, Swango sought to reestablish himself in life. But it wasn't long into his marriage with Rita that cracks began to emerge in the relationship. Swango and Rita Dumas had carried on for years as an unmarried couple just fine, but once they were married and living under the same roof day after day, night after night, the difficulties surfaced.

According to Rita, despite her many years of courtship, she knew almost immediately after the wedding that she had made a terrible mistake. And so, in January of 1991, less than two years after tying the knot, the two were separated and heading towards a finalized divorce. Shortly before his marriage to Rita, Swango had begun work as a lab technician at one of Virginia's premier coal companies, Aticoal Services, where his job was to test coal before it was shipped off to overseas clients. At first Swango appeared to be an ideal employee, and he was a personal favorite of the company's president, William C. Banks.

But shortly after his marriage crumbled, so too did Swango's behavior on the job. And soon enough, his coworkers began to exhibit the same telltale signs of poisoning that had followed Swango's toxic trail wherever he went. After his divorce was finalized in May of 1991, Swango was moving on again. Back in Ohio, he applied for admission to the Ohio Valley Medical Center. All of his applications in Virginia having been rejected, Swango decided it was time to lie his way out of his problems. Drawing upon his previous experience in fabrication, he submitted a completely fraudulent application in which he claimed that his license had been suspended due to a felony battery conviction over a fistfight at a local restaurant.

There was of course no mention of poison, and no mention of all the patients and colleagues who had been left either dead or severely ill by his actions. Swango laid it on thick, and his sob story of being in the wrong place at the wrong time and falling victim to a heavy-handed judge who had it in for him managed to win over his prospective employers. Hospital director Dr. Jeffrey Schultz was soon chomping at the bit to bring Swango on board and "give the young man a second chance."

But Swango had gone a little too far with his deception. He had even meticulously created false legal documents, such as a fake prison discharge sheet and a similarly forged docketing statement. He used these falsified documents to support his claims that he had been imprisoned over a minor fistfight in a restaurant, rather than the premeditated poisoning of his colleagues. In his sheer audacity, he even went so far as to type up a letter from the governor of Virginia stating that the governor had moved to completely restore all of Swango's rights as a citizen. But these very documents led Dr. Schultz to become suspicious that Swango was not quite what he claimed to be.

As his doubts began to build, he reached out to the police in Quincy, Illinois, to find out the truth. The results of these conversations were twofold: Dr. Schultz immediately suspended Swango's application process, and the authorities in Illinois were alerted to the fact that Swango was apparently forging documents, a serious criminal offense. Prosecutors began exploring the possibility of charging Swango with forgery, but by the time they had built a solid case against him, he had already moved on.

Incredibly enough, Swango had applied and been accepted at the University of South Dakota with the same forged documents that Dr. Schultz had uncovered. It was during this same period, in the summer of 1991, that Swango met a young nurse named Kristin Kinney. Kristin was engaged to a local doctor name Jerome Provenzano, but she was immediately enamored by the attention and charm that Swango showered her with. Feeling that he was offering her a lot more than what Dr. Provenzano was offering her, she eventually called off her engagement and began to see Swango full time instead.

When the two grew serious, Kristin's parents wanted to meet the man she was so smitten with, so the two arranged for them to have dinner together. For the most part, her parents were just as impressed with Swango as Kristin was, but there were a few areas of concern. They picked up on the fact that there were about three years of Swango's life that he could not account for: From about 1984 to 1987, he drew a complete blank. It seemed almost like he had amnesia. These were, of course, the years that Swango had been incarcerated for poisoning his coworkers. The other thing that bothered Kristin's parents was the fact that Swango supplied so little information on his own parents and family.

He was the most forthcoming about his father's background, detailing his military career and service in glowing terms. But about his mother he said next to nothing at all. He simply told them that she had grown ill and was living in a nursing home in Missouri. This was in fact true. A part of Muriel had died on the day that her son was convicted, and she had never fully recovered. Shortly after Swango went to prison, she had developed an acute case of Alzheimer's that was deemed bad enough for her to be placed in an assisted living center. Many believe that it was the stress of her son's conviction that sent her over the edge.

Not only that, after Muriel refused to pony up for his appeal, Swango had washed his hands of her completely and had no plans of seeing her ever again. Even though they didn't know the details of the divide, this obvious disconnect with his own family was something that greatly troubled Kristin's parents. But Kristin, who viewed her new man with the tunnel vision of love, could see no wrong. Despite her family's misgivings, the couple was engaged to be married in May of 1992. Kristin's mother expressed their feelings of confused foreboding best when she stated, "This is either the most wonderful thing in the world for Kristin, or he's some kind of nut."

The Truth Comes Out

For Michael Swango, 1992 seemed to be a comeback year. Against all odds he had managed to gain a residency at the University of South Dakota, and he was happily engaged to a beautiful young woman who adored him. They both moved to the state capital, Sioux Falls, and both found jobs at Royal C. Johnson Veterans Memorial Hospital. Kristin worked as a nurse in the intensive care unit while Swango was serving out the first rotation of his new residency at the same facility.

They tried at first to keep their relationship a secret, but the two were seen talking together on multiple occasions, and it soon became clear to Kristin's coworkers that she had a relationship with the new resident doctor. Kristin confided in one of her colleagues at the nursing station that she was indeed engaged to be married to Dr. Swango. Shortly after Kristin's revelation, Swango completed his rotation in the ICU and moved on to other sections of the medical campus. By all accounts, things were going well.

At this point, there were no mysterious illnesses following at Swango's heels, and he actually seemed to be doing a really good job as a doctor. There were no more fabricated five-minute H & P charts; this time he was doing things by the book. Even to an observer privy to Swango's previously tumultuous and questionable history, it would have seemed that Swango was really trying to turn his life around. Those who didn't know his past were immediately convinced that Swango was nothing other than what he claimed to be: a competent and hardworking doctor with no troubling history at all.

Swango may even have convinced himself of this false narrative, because in his increasing hubris, he actually sent in an application to the American Medical Association. It seems rather incredible that Swango wouldn't know that an application to the AMA might raise all of the old red flags he had tried so hard to bury, and in fact he soon realized his error and tried to withdraw his application. But it was too late. Not only the AMA reject him; they immediately contacted the administration at Royal C. Johnson Veterans Memorial Hospital.

It was now the middle of November, 1992, and the administrators at the South Dakota campus were growing increasingly alarmed about what they were hearing about their new doctor. They discovered that not only had he been convicted of poisoning coworkers, he was also suspected of causing the deaths of patients at OSU. This was obviously too much for them to accept, and they determined that Swango would have to go. This revelation occurred right before Thanksgiving, however, and so they decided to wait until after the holiday to let Dr. Swango know what they had found out.

They wanted to keep the matter quiet while they decided exactly what to do. But in an instance of incredible irony, right when they were trying to quietly sweep their findings under the rug, the Discovery Channel aired a documentary about the Swango case on their true crime series *Justice Files*. Several doctors, nurses, and other members of the hospital's medical staff saw this episode and recognized Dr. Swango.

Bear in mind that this was 1992, the year before the September that never ended and long before Google would become a household name. Nowadays a simple Google search will reveal just about everything you want to know about a person, but in 1992 it took a nationally syndicated television program for the folks in faraway Sioux Falls to learn what Dr. Swango had been convicted of in Illinois, and what he was suspected of doing in Ohio. This revelatory episode of *Justice Files* detonated a gigantic gossip bomb at the nurses' station, with everyone running in every direction to proclaim what they had heard about Dr. Swango.

In the aftermath of the explosion, Dr. Anthony Salem, the director of the hospital's medical residency program, quickly moved to cancel Swango's access to the pharmacy and terminate his status as a resident. Dr. Salem then contacted Swango and informed him that he didn't have to report to his next shift. He asked to meet him the next day at around two in the afternoon. Swango showed up to the meeting with a very nervous Kristin in tow and tried to play dumb, acting like he had no idea what all the fuss was about.

Even when Dr. Salem popped a recording of the *Justice Files* episode into the VCR, Swango still acted indignant and incredulous about the whole affair. He claimed to have no knowledge of any investigations begin conducted into his work at Ohio State, and he stuck to his story that his conviction for poisoning his colleagues had been a great miscarriage of justice in which he was completely railroaded by a biased judge and prosecution.

But for Kristin, the video was a revelation. She had had no inkling of any of this dark history until she saw it presented to her in Dr. Salem's office on his videotaped copy of that fateful episode of *Justice Files*. She remained quiet but visibly agitated during the meeting. But whatever she did, the end result of the encounter was going to be the same. Dr. Swango was ordered to tender his resignation by December 4, 1992.

Just a Little Bit of Charm

Following his forced resignation, Swango hired an attorney named Dennis McFarland in January of 1993. This lawyer worked as Swango's counsel during the final suspension hearings held at the end of the month. As the hearings came to a close, McFarland suggested that Swango contact Vern Cook, who was the president of the hospital employees union. McFarland believed that since Swango had occasionally worked at the local VA during his residency, he could be classified as a federal employee, thereby making him eligible for the federal protections that this would provide.

Swango and Cook met in person a handful of times before Cook agreed to take on his case. Over the next few weeks Swango bonded with Cook, who was a fellow former soldier and a Vietnam veteran. The two would spend countless hours together at Cook's house engaging in what they called "strategy sessions." At times they would be up all night and into the early morning hours rifling through legal documents and discussing just how they should handle Swango's case.

While Cook and Swango were deliberating, Kristin was becoming more and more unglued. She wanted to stand by Swango's side, but the increased scrutiny of the media, who now followed Swango's every movement, with photographers literally jumping out of the bushes at them, was making it much harder to do so. And in the cold winter days of early February, she reached a breaking point. It was at this time that she reached out to a former colleague, a fellow nurse named Lynette Mueller, for help. Meeting up with Mueller at a popular local hangout called Champs, Kristin expressed her frustration with the situation, saying point blank, "I need out." She then asked Mueller if she could perhaps live with her and her husband for a while. She also revealed that Swango had been discussing the idea of moving overseas so that he could work somewhere far away from the charges that were being leveled at him.

The fact that Swango was already making such plans is very telling, since he would later make good on just such a strategy. But Kristin never did move in with her friend Mueller. Instead of getting away from it all, she sought to stem her growing anxiety by self-medicating. She began to take Prozac and to drink heavily just to get through the day. In addition to what she was doing to herself through medication and alcohol, she also had a suspicion that Swango was slipping her a little something as well. She began to have strange headaches out of nowhere, and she grew even more apprehensive when she realized that some of the symptoms she was experiencing were the same as those of Swango's previous victims.

Probably due to a combination of all of these things, Kristin felt like she was losing her mind. And on a cold night in late February 1993, when the police found the young woman taking a walk down a busy Sioux Falls street without any clothes on, they too realized that something was very wrong with Kristin Kinney. This incident of walking completely naked in the cold bought her an immediate ticket to the psych ward of Charter Hospital. She remained there for about four days before she was deemed stable enough to be released.

Kristin spent the next few weeks complaining of her headaches and heartache before she finally packed up her things and hopped into her pickup truck to head back to her parents in Virginia. When she got there her aunt offered to put her up in an apartment that she rented out in the town of Portsmouth, just across the Elizabeth River from Norfolk. Kristin's mom and stepfather felt that their prayers had been answered when Kristin came back to Virginia, but less than two weeks later this dream turned into a nightmare when Swango resurfaced as well.

When Kristin's mother answered to her door on April 23, 1993, she was dismayed to see Swango standing arm in arm with her daughter. They were apparently reunited once again. During Swango's brief stay with Kristin in Virginia he once again sent out a rapid-fire burst of applications to hospitals and medical centers for residency, and amazingly he received a response, this time for a psychiatric position at the State University of New York at Stony Brook on Long Island. Swango hoped that a location so far removed from Sioux Falls, North Dakota, would enable him to shed some of the excess baggage of his past.

Swango's application was received and reviewed by Dr. Alan Miller, the director of the resident psychiatry department. Dr. Miller immediately arranged for an in-person interview with Swango on April 27th. Also present were the department chair and one of the faculty members. As the interview began, it seemed to be going exceedingly well. The group was impressed with Swango's easy personality, his obvious intelligence and his graceful charm. But then Swango dropped his bombshell by informing them, "I have to tell you, I've served time in jail. I want you to know that."

Swango then brought up the same old lie he had used in South Dakota: that he had been incarcerated not for poisoning his colleagues, but for his part in a barroom brawl. Swango then pulled out the same bogus legal documents he had shown in South Dakota in order to bolster his claim. Fortunately for Swango, but rather unfortunately for the general public, Miller and his colleagues readily accepted Swango's story. His staff did a cursory check of Swango's references, but the superficial correspondence between the institutions failed to bring up any red flags, and without further ado Swango was accepted into the program on June 1, 1993.

Before he left for New York, on June 20th, Swango and Kristin had dinner with her parents. It was supposed to be a Father's Day celebration for Kristin's stepfather, Al Cooper. But Swango seemed to think it was a congratulatory dinner for him instead, and he treated it as such, going on and on for most of the night about how great it was that he had been accepted in New York. In light of the recent drama surrounding his sudden dismissal from Royal C. Johnson Veterans Memorial Hospital, Al was a little more skeptical about Swango's prospects, however. He asked him, "Michael, after all of these problems, what if they hear about them?"

Absolutely beaming with confidence, Swango was quick to dismiss Al's concern, cheerfully chirping, "What they don't know, they don't know." Swango then left his fiancée and her family behind for what would be his third attempt to finish his residency since he had graduated from med school nearly a decade ago in 1983. Swango was hoping that the third time would be the charm—but in the end his actions would be a little bit less than charming.

The Road to Destruction

Swango officially began his residency at Stony Brook on July 1, 1993, moving into a dormitory that was provided for hospital residents. Swango's first patient at the hospital was a man named Dominic Buffalino. Buffalino was well-known in his community; he was a World War Two veteran and a longtime organizer for the Long Island Republican Party. He had come to the hospital for a mild case of lung congestion. His family believed it was nothing more than a bad cold bug, but at his age they didn't want to take any chances.

Buffalino was in good spirits when he first met the new resident doctor, Michael Swango—or as Swango had introduced himself, Dr. Kirk. Swango, a longtime Star Trek fan, had decided to go by an alias during this residency, perhaps hoping that confusion over his name might just throw investigators off the trail should there be trouble. After meeting the patient, Swango was then introduced to his wife, Teresa, who was very impressed by the doctor's bedside manner. She found him to be very "pleasant and reassuring."

But his reassuring tone would completely flat line on her the very next morning when Swango himself telephoned to coldly deliver the news, "I'm sorry to inform you that your husband is dead." Teresa was instantly beside herself with grief, as if someone had just stabbed her in the heart. Swango, however, playing his strange, warped and sadistic game, seemed like a cat cruelly toying with its captured mouse as he milked the experience for what it was worth. He kept telling Dominic Buffalino's distraught wife, "Stay on the phone. Don't hang up. Talk to me."

When Teresa came to the hospital, accompanied by Dominic's brother Andrew, Swango was there, standing next to the bedside of Theresa's deceased husband. She broke down into tears once again as Swango offered his bizarre explanation of how a patient suffering from pneumonia had spontaneously expired.

Not a whole lot is known about how Swango spent the rest of his first two weeks at Stony Brook; the next significant incident occurred on July 14th, when he called Kristin back in Virginia. It has never been entirely clear what went on during this conversation, but Kristin's next-door neighbor couldn't help hearing the result of it as Kristin's hysterical crying and shouting filtered through the thin walls of the apartment. Shortly after the neighbor heard this disturbance, Kristin placed a call to her mother. She seemed strangely detached and devoid of emotion. Sensing that something was gravely wrong, her mother pleaded with Kristin to come stay with her, but Kristin finally ended the labored and halting conversation by telling her, "No, Mom, I'm fine. I love you."

Kristin's mother knew that she wasn't fine. She was extremely worried, telling her husband, "There's something terribly wrong with Kristin." Her husband didn't quite share her concern, though. Figuring that she was just overreacting, he told her, "She's 27 years old. Give her some space." She tried to take this advice, but then Swango himself called from New York and told her that she should probably check on Kristin because she had sounded pretty upset. Oddly enough, the same mother who had been ready to drop everything to check on her distraught daughter suddenly made a full reversal.

She didn't want to admit to Swango that Kristin had seemed rattled, and so she lied to him, "She's calmed down." Perhaps she suspected that Swango had broken up with Kristin and didn't want to give Swango the satisfaction of knowing that he had broken her daughter's heart. But whatever the case may be, her first intuition was right: Kristin was in fact in dire need of an intervention. Sadly, no one did intervene on her behalf, and the next night her parents received a phone call from the police requesting that they come down to the station in regard to an incident involving their daughter.

They didn't give any details, but shortly after arriving at the police station the couple learned the horrible news. Kristin had been found dead, slumped against a tree. She had apparently taken her own life. Had Kristin committed suicide? Was she capable of such an act? It seemed she was: she left behind extensive journal entries and notes in her own hand that documented her mental decline and her decision to end it all.

One note addressed to her parents read as follows: "I love you both so much. I just didn't want to be here anymore. Just found day to day living a constant struggle with my thoughts. I'd say I'm sorry but I'm not. I feel that sense of peace, 'peace of mind', I've been looking for. It's nice. I'll be seeing you!"

Sadly, these were the last expressions and sentiments that Kristin's family would have from her.

There could be no doubt that she had indeed committed suicide, but the family still couldn't help but wonder if it was the constant psychological pushing and shoving from Swango that had driven her there.

New York, New York

Dr. Swango's next apparent victim during his tenure at Stony Brook was Barron Harris, who checked into the hospital on September 29, 1993. The patient was a 60-year-old man who, aside from the bout of pneumonia that had led to his admission, was a fairly healthy individual. That is, until he was assigned to a certain resident doctor named Michael Swango. Just as was the case with the ill-fated Dominic Buffalino, the Harris family was initially quite impressed with Swango, who seemed to be the epitome of the selfless, caring doctor. Swango appeared to devote all of his time to ensuring that his patients were being cared for properly.

According to Barron's wife, the other doctors always seemed to be in too much of a hurry to engage with family members. Swango, however, took the time to listen to them and assuage their fears and concerns. But her main concern soon became Dr. Swango himself. Just a few days later she found her husband on a respirator and unresponsive, and all Swango would say was the alarming statement, "I hope it's nothing I did". Swango then argued with the grieving wife, coldly challenging her wish to keep her husband alive, by flatly informing her, "He's in a coma, and I know he's not coming out of it. He's already suffered brain damage." He then badgered the poor woman into signing her husband's death warrant in the form of a DNR (Do Not Resuscitate) directive.

While these events were transpiring in New York, back in Virginia, Kristin's still grieving mother had begun corresponding with one of Kristin's former coworkers at the hospital in South Dakota. It was through these exchanges that personnel in South Dakota were tipped off to Swango's latest residency in New York.

When this news reached the dean of the University of South Dakota Medical Center, he in turn alerted the dean of Stony Brook, Jordan Cohen. After hearing all of the disturbing details of Swango's previous history, Cohen immediately notified the department chair, who then sent the word out to the man who had brought Swango to Stony Brook in the first place, Dr. Alan Miller. Dr. Miller arranged an immediate meeting with Swango to question him about the allegations.

Swango, apparently knowing that he was cornered, readily admitted that he had indeed been convicted of poisoning his coworkers. But he adamantly maintained that he was innocent of the charges.

Dr. Miller, however, had had enough of Swango's excuses. He promptly informed him that his residency was going to be suspended. Swango wouldn't let up, though, and like a man obsessed, he found his way to Miller's office once again the next day and began pleading for some form of leniency. While Miller was not prepared to let him stay at Stony Brook, he did offer Swango some advice: "Go somewhere that really needs a doctor, somewhere that's desperate."

Miller was suggesting that Swango make a trip overseas to some impoverished region of the developing world where competent doctors were a scarce resource. Programs such as Doctors Without Borders do indeed exist to let doctors lend a helping hand in far-flung parts of the globe. The doctors who participate in these programs have various reasons for doing so. Some do it so that their student loans will be forgiven, others do it out of a sincere wish to help others, some crave the adventure of the overseas experience—and some hope that the needy host country will overlook some slip-up or negligence that has left them unable to find work in their home country. Dr. Miller was suggesting that Swango fit into this last category and should explore such an avenue as his last chance to get back into medicine.

Shortly after this meeting, the Stony Brook dean, Jordan Cohen, fired off warning letters to every single medical school in the nation. The letters detailed Swango's troubled background and advised them not to consider his applications. Swango had been essentially blacklisted from every hospital in the United States. If he ever wanted to work in medicine again, he basically had no choice but to leave the country to do it.

Swango tried to lay low after leaving Stony Brook, heading south to stay with a friend of his in Atlanta. But it wasn't long before the FBI, which now had an ongoing investigation into his misdeeds, was on his trail. In February of 1994 they tracked him down to Atlanta—and were deeply concerned to find that he had landed a job at a wastewater plant. Fearing that Swango might have the opportunity to poison the water supply, the FBI determined that they had to act. They immediately alerted the waste treatment facility about Swango's past, and he was accordingly dismissed from the company on July 22, 1994.

But despite the diligent investigation, the slow bureaucracy that often plagues the Bureau meant that the FBI didn't get around to issuing a warrant for Michael Swango's arrest until October 27, 1994. It was a little too late. Swango, apparently having taken Dr. Miller's advice to heart, had decided to take his career overseas. He would soon be thousands of miles away in the sunny African republic of Zimbabwe.

The Homicidal Medical Missionary

Michael Swango arrived in Zimbabwe in November of 1994. Even as the FBI's dragnet was closing in on him, he had managed to establish contact with the director of a little-known Zimbabwean hospital called the Mnene Mission through an overseas job agency called Options. This agency's main mission was to fill medical positions in other countries with American doctors. The director, a man named Christopher Zshiri, was at first greatly impressed with Swango's credentials—but the more he witnessed the doctor in the field, the more he realized that he seemed woefully unprepared for even some of the most basic tasks.

Swango attempted to chalk up this lack of general knowledge to the fact that he had previously been practicing in the highly specialized field of neurosurgery and did not have much experience outside of it. In reality, Swango was clumsy in certain areas simply because he had never been able to hold a job long enough to gain the experience that he should have had at this point in his career. But Dr. Zshiri was an easygoing and understanding man, and he simply took Swango's word for it.

He also came up with a way to erase Swango's ineptitude: He instructed him to take a 5-month position as an intern at Mpilo Hospital in nearby Bulawayo, a historic city that is the second largest in Zimbabwe. Ever since the 1980s, Mpilo Hospital has been a major treatment center for AIDS patients. And in late 1994 when Swango arrived, they were in desperate need of extra medical help for the massive influx of those affected by the disease.

It was for this reason—as well as Swango's amiable bedside manner—that Mpilo's superintendent, Dr. Chaibva, was so excited to bring him on board. He was also quite impressed with the seemingly boundless energy that Swango exhibited. Just as he had during his days as an EMT, Swango seemed to be able to work literally round the clock on 24-hour shifts without any sleep. At Mpilo Hospital, Swango put on his best face for the medical staff, and according to most he did a stellar job. There were some who had their doubts, however.

Many wondered why this skilled American doctor would leave the comfort of the United States, where he could make a ton of money, for third-world Zimbabwe, where he made next to nothing. These skeptics were not quite sold on the explanation that Swango generally supplied, which was that he was there for purely altruistic purposes—that he just wanted to make the world a better place. To them, it seemed that there had to be some hidden motive.

One of Swango's most skeptical colleagues was Abdi Mesbah, a doctor on loan from Iran. In fact, Dr. Mesbah may have been a little *too* skeptical; he even went so far as to explain Swango's medical inexpertness by claiming that he was an agent working for the CIA! But most Mpilo staff dismissed this theory as absurd anti-Americanism, and besides Dr. Mesbah and a few other dissenters, the general consensus was that Swango was telling them the truth and simply wanted to be part of a good cause.

Swango's main go-to guy while he was at Mpilo Hospital was a 27-year-old staffer named Ian Lorimer. Ian was a welcoming guide who showed Swango the ins and outs of the hospital. The two worked long shifts together, and Ian helped Swango develop the necessary experience in some of the more basic areas of general practice treatment. The two hit it off well together and seemed to be almost the best of friends. The only time that

Swango really rubbed Lorimer wrong was when he used excessive profanity. Lorimer and his wife, Cheryl, were both devout Christians; they even headed a bible study group at the Bulawayo Central Presbyterian Church.

Although Swango had been in the habit of unbridled "locker room talk" during his paramedic days, he was able to switch off this more abrasive side of his personality out of respect for Lorimer. He even showed an interest in Christianity, attending Sunday services with Lorimer and his wife. The two continued to be close friends until Swango's time at Mpilo came to a close in May of 1995. It was near the end of his term at this hospital he had grown to enjoy that Swango first expressed some disdain about the job he was going to be doing.

He was leaving a modern hospital in Zimbabwe's second largest city and going back to a low-budget, ill-equipped, substandard facility in the middle of nowhere. Swango quietly told himself that after he finished his contract at the Mnene Mission, he would return to Bulawayo and his friends at Mpilo Hospital. But besides his dissatisfaction, there was another factor in whether or not Swango could successfully finish his term at Mnene Mission: the pesky problem that as soon as he arrived, people started to die.

Killers Can't be Choosers

Swango returned to Mnene Mission with his own diabolical mission ready to launch, and he soon left a string of victims in his wake, all of whom died of mysterious causes.

The first of these mysterious deaths was Rhoda Mahlamvana. This woman dropped dead for seemingly no reason shortly after Swango paid a visit. Swango was right on the scene afterwards as well, preparing her death certificate before her body was even cold. Rhoda had come in for relatively minor burns, and how she could suddenly die like that would become an enduring mystery.

The next odd incident involving Dr. Swango was the case of Keneas Mzezewa. Swango approached Keneas while he was slumbering, then woke him up to give him an injection. This injection almost completely paralyzed Keneas, but right before his lungs seized up on him, he managed to hiss out the words, "Dr. Mike gave me an injection!" As fellow staff members looked on, Swango resorted to his old tactic of claiming that the patient was delusional. He adamantly denied the charge and retorted that Keneas was obviously hallucinating and had imagined the whole thing.

But while the word of one person can be easily dismissed, the word of several witnesses is much harder to ignore. And on June 26th, Katazo Shavo, who was recovering from surgery on his leg, had his whole family with him to witness the peculiar "extra treatments" Dr. Swango delivered to his patients.

Swango arrived on the scene to find Katazo's relatives huddled around his bedside. In order to administer his handiwork, he requested that they leave the room. Swango then closed the curtains around the man's bed and got to work. But even though they could no longer see what was happening to their relative, they could hear his screams. They later described his cries as akin to those of a wild animal. Moments later, they saw Dr. Swango rush out of the room without saying a word.

The family quickly reentered Katazo's room and found him still crying out in intense pain. Then he told them with the kind of certainty that only the imminent specter of death can bring, "We won't go home together because I am going to die. The doctor has injected me with something, and I think I am going to die. I won't get home. I am going to die." The family reassured him and left, but when they returned later that evening, they were stopped by a nurse who confirmed what Katazo himself had predicted: He was dead. There was no explanation, no reason; just a family who saw their loved one laughing and smiling one second, and then, after Dr. Swango left his side, dying a horrible death the next.

Dr. Swango was busy, and now apparently really in the swing of things with his murderous routine. The very next day, on June 27th, he found his next victim, a local farmer named Phillimon Chipoko. The whole thing happened right under his wife's nose. It was late at night in the hospital, and Phillimon was already sleeping his bed. Just a few minutes later his wife, Yeudzirai, would be asleep as well, dozing off in the chair next to her husband's bedside. She only drifted back to wakefulness when she heard the door of the room open and saw Dr. Swango go over to her husband and tinker with his IV.

Yeudzirai snapped back to consciousness several minutes later as a nurse shook her awake and asked bluntly, "Did anyone tell you your husband is dead?" The patient had apparently expired with his corpse curled up in bed as if he were still asleep. But this "sleeper" would never wake up again.

As was commonplace with Swango, despite the mounting evidence that something wasn't right, the hospital administrators didn't dare think that their new doctor was the one causing the problems. And if it wasn't for some quick-thinking nurses, Swango would have claimed another victim in July. Virginia Sibanda was in the maternity ward expecting to have a baby at any moment when she crossed paths with the doctor of death himself, Michael Swango. On July 7th, Swango was assigned to evaluate the stage and condition of Virginia's pregnancy. After a cursory examination, he noted that she was dilating and progressing through her labor well and told her that he did not expect any complications.

Swango returned a few hours later and injected a syringe of pink liquid into Virginia's IV. She noted that he seemed to be trying to inject the liquid quickly, before the nurses turned to see what he was doing. It was as if he didn't want anyone to see it—but Virginia saw it, and she wouldn't forget it. Shortly thereafter, she experienced excruciating pain in her abdomen and felt her baby react violently inside of her. She then had a feverish sensation like she was boiling from the inside out.

Virginia screamed for help and asked for the nurses to douse her in cold water because of the unbearable heat she felt. The concerned nurses dutifully fulfilled her request by covering her in cold compresses. As soon as they were able to calm her down enough, they asked about the cause of her distress. Virginia told them that "Dr. Mike" (as many of the patients at the mission called Swango) had injected her with something just before the onset of the unbearable pain that the entire nursing staff had seen her go through.

It is no coincidence that no matter where Swango went to perpetrate his acts, it was usually the nursing staff who caught on to his depredations before anyone else. They were the ones most often on site with the patients. They know who comes and goes, and who does what, better than anyone else. And in Zimbabwe, just like in America, they were the first to realize that something was definitely not right about Dr. Michael Swango.

Swango did have one defender, however, a nurse's aide by the name of Edith Ngwenya. While the others gossiped openly about the possibility of Swango having a sinister agenda, Edith always rejected such claims. She reminded them that someone like Swango had sacrificed much to come to Zimbabwe to help them. He wouldn't come all the way to Zimbabwe just to kill people, right? That would be ridiculous, right? At least, that was young Edith's logic. Not believing that Swango could be capable of such things, she felt that the nurses' complaints against him were based on nothing more than their own petty jealousies and personal resentments.

But even this defender would desert Swango when she too developed a mystery illness and suddenly and inexplicably dropped dead just a few days later. Apparently Swango had such little control over his murderous compulsions that he couldn't resist killing even when it meant eradicating one of the few people who would have continued to shield him from blame. It appears that Swango was an equal opportunity murderer who struck whenever the opportunity presented itself, killing friend and foe alike.

Swango's Last Chance

It was midsummer under the hot Zimbabwe sun, and the dead bodies had been piling up at the Mnene Mission ever since Dr. Swango's arrival in May. The hospital administration either did not know the full extent of what was happening or was not willing to think the unthinkable when it came to Swango's true character. But on July 20, 1995, an incident occurred that forced them to confront what was happening.

Thirty-five-year-old Margaret Zhou had come into the mission after enduring a nearly full-term miscarriage. Medical staff treated her pain with medication and then worked to remove the fetal remains from her womb. The procedure seemed to have been completed without any complications, yet later that day Margaret was found to be deceased. Incredibly alarmed that a healthy woman who had undergone a routine procedure had died for no apparent reason, mission director Dr. Zshiri began to question the hospital staff about what had happened.

After some digging, he obtained the testimony of a maternity nurse who informed him not of what had happened to Margaret Zhou, but of what she had witnessed with Virginia Sibanda. She explained to Dr. Zshiri that the patient had claimed that "Dr. Mike" had injected her with something. Hearing this story for the first time, Dr. Zshiri immediately went to Virginia's bedside and personally questioned her about what had happened. Still quite shaken up by the event, she recounted what she had experienced in great detail.

Dr. Zshiri was greatly disturbed to hear this account, but he was even more alarmed when shortly thereafter another nurse came forward and relayed the story of Keneas Mzezewa, whom Swango had woken up and given a shot that paralyzed his whole body and nearly took his life. Dr. Zshiri then interviewed this man as well, and after he recounted his horrific tale, Keneas offered up the statement, "I do not understand what happened—but I nearly lost my life." He also informed Dr. Zshiri that he was still terrified of Swango and feared that he might come back to finish him off.

Sensing Keneas's sincerity, Dr. Zshiri began to fear for him as well, and so he had him transferred to the neighboring Mzume Mission Hospital until he could figure out just what was going on with his new American doctor. Deeply concerned Dr. Zshiri contacted the Lutheran church headquarters and spoke with the director, Howard Mpofu. After taking in the disturbing news, the director instructed him to contact Dr. David Dhakama, the superintendent for the whole region and Dr. Zshiri's immediate supervisor, to inform him of what was happening.

Upon hearing the story, Dr. Dhakama didn't waste any time in bringing the police onto the case. The police soon obtained a search warrant for Swango's living quarters. When they got there, they encountered Swango outside speaking with a staff member. Informing him of the warrant, they ordered him to step aside as they searched his room. The first thing they noticed was that Swango's clothes were strewn all over the place. The second was the huge stockpile of pharmaceuticals, syringes and vials of chemicals that Swango had amassed.

When the police reemerged from Swango's quarters, Dr. Dhakama personally informed Swango that his license to practice medicine in Zimbabwe would be temporarily suspended and all privileges revoked until he was cleared in the investigation. Then, on October 13th, Lutheran Church representative Howard Mpofu arrived at Swango's door and personally handed him a letter announcing his termination from the Mnene Mission.

Probably unsure of where else he could run to, Swango went to the only other place he knew in Zimbabwe, the city of Bulawayo, his old training grounds where he had spent his first five months in the country. There he contacted Ian Lorimer and informed him of his plight (at least from his own warped perspective). Ian, wishing to help his friend, directed him to a human rights lawyer named David Coltart. This attorney had quite an illustrious career at this point, and Ian figured if anyone could help Swango, Coltart could.

Swango met up with Coltart in his downtown law office on August 23, 1995, to discuss his options. Coltart, like so many others, was convinced by Swango's demeanor that he was a sincere individual who had been unfairly treated. Coltart was used to fighting all manner of human rights abuses in the iron-clad dictatorship of Zimbabwe's Robert Mugabe, and he could easily believe that Swango was indeed being subject to some sort of discrimination. Coltart was a champion ready for a righteous cause, but unfortunately he wouldn't find any such thing in Swango's case.

Swango was more than ready to latch onto the narrative that he had been singled out for unfair treatment as the only American doctor at the clinic. The defense seemed tailor-made to shield himself from his own diabolical indiscretions. As a devout Presbyterian, Swango's friend Ian Lorimer was also quick to accept that Swango had been wronged by the Lutheran Mnene Mission, and he was ready to fight on his friend's behalf as well. Fully championing the cause, he even went to the director of

Mpilo Hospital in Bulawayo, Dr. Chaibva, and petitioned him to hire Swango and restore his privileges to practice medicine.

Dr. Chaibva was a cautious administrator, however. He wanted to know why Swango had been suspended from the Mnene Mission in the first place, so he contacted Dr. Zshiri to ask him personally. But when he raised the question of whether he should take Swango on board at Mpilo, all Dr. Zshiri would say was, "If I were you, I would not employ him." And when Dr. Chaibva asked him to explain this cryptic remark, Dr. Zshiri would only tell him, "It's under investigation."

Dr. Zshiri doubtless didn't feel at liberty to discuss the details until the investigation had run its course. But without any other information, Dr. Chaibva figured that the suspension was probably due to a personal dispute that the director did not wish to get into, rather than any medical negligence on Swango's part. And so, despite Dr. Zshiri's warning, Dr. Chaibva took this as his own personal green light to restore Swango's privileges and hire him at Mpilo Hospital. He would end up regretting this decision for the rest of his life.

Swango's reign of terror at Mpilo Hospital began shortly after he was reinstated and began working at the facility. With nowhere else to stay, Swango was actually given a spare room in the hospital itself. With this kind of 24-hour access it was easier than ever for him to administer his lethal injections to patients. It was quite unlike the open-air environment of the Mnene Mission, where he was almost constantly within earshot of or being observed by someone. At Mpilo, Swango could plot his murders at leisure from the privacy of his sleeping quarters, making sure that no one ever heard or saw a thing.

But while there were no longer any witnesses to his crimes, there were still plenty of mysterious deaths. The first of these was a patient who came in for routine hernia treatment and then just up and died in the early morning hours of the next day. Another patient, who had drunk hydrochloric acid in a botched suicide attempt resulting in severe burning of the tissue in his throat and stomach, died under similarly strange conditions. It can be surmised that Swango decided to help finish what the suicidal patient had started, because just a few days later, the patient was dead—not from his injuries, but with the same calling cards as all the other strange deaths that followed Swango around.

These mysterious deaths continued, but in the hustle and bustle of the busy hospital, they were mostly overlooked. Then a reporter from the local newspaper, the *Bulawayo Chronicle*, tracked Swango down to Mpilo Hospital, and Swango was back in the spotlight once again.

Journalists had been asking around with hospital staff for a while, but they usually hit a brick wall of silence. On this particular day, however, a reporter named Foster Dongozi just happened to be in the right place at the right time. He was in the middle of asking the hospital's switchboard operator to page Dr. Swango when Swango himself walked right up behind him and told him, "I'm Dr. Swango. Can I help you?" Surprised to actually bump into Swango in person, Dongozi turned around and said, "My name is Foster Dongozi, and I'm a reporter for the *Chronicle*."

Swango was taken aback by this statement. Looking incredibly nervous and uncomfortable, he began to back away. He lifted an arm as if to defend himself as he managed to choke out, "I can't answer that. Talk to my lawyer!" He then literally ran from the scene, with half the hospital staff staring after him. But instead of going to Swango's lawyer, the reporter went straight to Swango's employer and launched an improvisational interview on an unsuspecting Dr. Chaibva.

He asked whether Swango was actually living at the hospital, and if he had indeed been investigated in the deaths of patients. Dr. Chaibva responded that he didn't know on both counts, but Dongozi suspected that he knew a whole lot more than he was telling. To be fair, the only information that Dr. Chaibva was withholding was his knowledge about where Swango lived. When it came to him being linked to the deaths of patients, Dr. Chaibva was just as much in the dark as everyone else. He still figured that Swango's dismissal from the Mnene Mission had been due to a personality conflict.

But now the heat was on, and he had been pushed too far; he had no choice but to launch his own personal investigation. He contacted Zimbabwe's Minister of Health and Child Welfare, Timothy Stamps, who told him everything he knew about why Swango had been expelled from the Mnene Mission, including the unsettling eyewitness accounts of the surviving patients. Dr. Chaibva had now heard enough, and in mid-March of 1996 he ordered Swango to meet him in a Mpilo Hospital conference room, where he promptly informed the expat doctor, "Your services are no longer required here."

Swango's Eviction Notice

On March 31, 1996, Michael Swango paid a visit to the estate of Lynette O'Hare. He had met her daughter Paulette through his bible study meetings with the Lorimers. During a brief discussion with Lynette, Swango was able to muster up enough of the old charm to convince this lady he barely knew to let him lodge with her. Paulette was moving to England, and Lynette figured she could use both the money and the company that Swango's presence would bring, but she didn't quite know what she was getting into.

Swango was currently dating another girl he had met at the Lorimers' bible study sessions, one LeeAnne, and he subsequently introduced her to Lynette. The relationship didn't last, however; LeeAnne broke it off shortly thereafter. After this breakup, Swango's mood changed completely. He went from being relatively pleasant and sociable to hiding in his room for days at a time. Growing increasingly concerned for her house guest, Lynette called up the Lorimers to see if she could get any insight about the situation.

It was during this phone call that Ian Lorimer confirmed that Swango was the same expat doctor Lynette had heard about on the news who was accused of "experimenting" on patients. Ian was quick to inform her, however, that the whole thing was a "put-up job" arranged to frame Swango. Lynette, who believed in many of the conspiracy theories and tales of persecution that were continually floating around Zimbabwe in those years, readily accepted this explanation. She knew that the corrupt government of Zimbabwe was capable of such human rights abuses and worse.

This is perhaps the great irony of a corrupt and draconian dictatorship such as those of Zimbabwe's Robert Mugabe and Iraq's Saddam Hussein. These heavy-handed leaders create a unique problem for themselves through their horrible human rights records, documented corruption, and their own non-existent credibility. When the regime itself is frequently abusing the public trust and persecuting the innocent, when someone like Michael Swango comes along, who really is a threat to the public, and the corrupt dictatorship calls him out as such, the public trust in that government is so lacking that no one believes the truth!

This was the very sweet spot in which Swango found himself under Robert Mugabe's hated regime. What made the story even sweeter to Lynette's ears was the fact that famed human rights lawyer David Coltart was representing Swango as legal counsel. Lynette assumed that if a respected attorney like Coltart believed in Swango enough to represent him, then he must be telling the truth. Figuring that she now understood Swango's plight a little better, she asked Ian to give Swango a call, in the hope that a pep talk from his friend could raise his spirits.

This strategy seemed to have worked. Whatever Ian said to Swango broke him out of his funk, and he came out of his room the next day to join Lynette for breakfast and morning tea. He even apologized for his odd behavior over the last few days and assured her that everything would be alright. Now apparently without a care in the world, Swango sailed through the rest of the spring without incident.

Then, as spring turned to summer, Swango was gratified to meet a new love interest in the person of Joanna Daly, a lifelong resident of Zimbabwe and recent divorcee. The two were introduced by a mutual friend at a dinner in June of 1996. Swango and Joanna hit it off almost immediately and soon were spending all of their time together. Although Daly had three children to care for, it became routine for her to drop her kids off at school, pick up Swango at Lynette's estate, and then drop him back off before she showed up at the school again to bring her children home. This evolved into Swango staying over not just during school hours but at all hours of the day. But the longer Swango stayed, the more ill at ease they all became—literally!

As was all too common in the life of Michael Swango, the longer he was around Joanna and her children, the more illness-prone they became. First her kids came down with what she thought was the flu or some other viral infection and were plagued with severe vomiting and diarrhea. Then, after one quiet night at home with Swango in which he offered her a simple cup of tea— a kind, caring action from anyone else, but deadly in Swango's book—Joanna too fell horribly ill, vomiting for hours before collapsing in bed and blacking out in exhaustion.

And Joanna's home wasn't the only one to be paid a visit by the poison fairy. From the accounts of Lynette O'Hare, it seems highly likely that she and her two maids were being poisoned as well. Lynette would spend the entire day vomiting sometimes, but she tried to pass it off as a particularly aggressive flu bug. Her maids, though, suspected that Swango was tampering with the food. In fact, they were fairly convinced that he was sneaking into their house, which was situated across from Lynette's main residence, and lacing certain foods with poison.

For example, on one occasion they had bought a brand-new jar of peanut butter. They had never opened the jar's seal. Yet one day they found the seal broken and the surface of the peanut butter looking like someone had pressed something down inside of it. (Such "tamper evident" seals exist to make sure no one has compromised our food and beverages, and this kind of incident just goes to show you why they're necessary!) The maids could clearly see that their peanut butter had been tampered with, so they threw it out lest they come down with some mystery illness from eating it. The women reported their findings to Lynette and were finally able to convince her that something was just not quite right about her house guest.

Soon after the peanut butter incident, the maids began to sleep inside the main house, right next to Lynette's room. This was partially out of their fear of Swango cornering them in their house, and partly out of a desire to protect Lynette by keeping an eye on her. During their nocturnal vigilance they saw Swango get up in the middle of the night, walk down the hall, and stand in front of Lynette's open door. He just stood there, for no apparent reason. Upon seeing this, one of the maids started making noise, clearing her throat and humming, to let him know they were still awake and paying attention. As soon as Swango heard this, he ran back into his room.

The behavior was so odd that the maids began to seriously fear for their lives. They wondered if Swango was planning on murdering them all in their sleep, and there wasn't a night after this that at least one of them didn't stay awake and keep watch. Living with Swango was proving to be quite a tiresome business, and Lynette O'Hare eventually had enough of his odd and frequently menacing behavior. On August 7, 1996, she told him that he would have to go. She had cooked up an excuse that her son was coming to town and needed to stay in the room Swango was using.

Initially she gave him two weeks' notice, but the following day she came home to him blasting music on her CD player and her entire house a wreck. She had had enough and ordered Swango to leave that very day, adding that she was going to change the locks and hire a security guard upon his departure. Swango marched out of Lynette's house and—so she hoped—out of her life for good.

But he didn't leave without a parting gift. The next day when Lynette tried to start her car, she discovered that the engine wouldn't even turn over; it would die as soon as she turned the key. She had to have the car towed to a mechanic, and his diagnosis provoked an immediate fury in her veins. A large amount of sugar had been deposited into the gas tank. Michael Swango had left his chemical calling card once again.

Skipping Bail and Skipping Town

After being kicked out of Lynette's house, Swango began to live with his girlfriend Joanna on a full time basis. His days now consisted mostly of following the latest developments in his case with his lawyer Coltart and lazily lounging around Joanna's house. Then one afternoon his repose was interrupted by a startling phone call from the police. They wanted to interview him in person.

Knowing that they wouldn't take no for an answer, Swango agreed to come in on August 29th. But even as he was setting the date, Swango had no intention of showing up. Under the pretense of wanting to go on a hiking trip to "get away from it all," Swango had Joanna drop him off at the Zimbabwean equivalent of a Greyhound bus station, a Blue Arrow terminal, on August 14th. He said he was going to the Nyanga National Park to walk in the mountainous and rugged terrain of this wilderness reserve in order to clear his mind before he faced the police.

August 29th came and went, and there was still no sign of Swango. Just a few weeks later, however, Swango resurfaced in Zambia with a job at the University Teaching Hospital in Lusaka, the country's capital. After about two months of uneventful employment, Zimbabwe sent out a bulletin notifying all of the countries in southwest Africa of the charges Swango was facing. Once the Zambians learned of Swango's background, they dropped him like a hot potato, officially firing him on November 19, 1996. Once again, he was forced to seek employment elsewhere.

Swango crossed over into neighboring Namibia. He was able to get some minor temporary work there, but he soon opted to head to South Africa, where he figured he would have more opportunity. Here he came into contact with a medical placement company and secured a position at a medical facility in Saudi Arabia. He was scheduled to begin work at the Royal Hospital in Dhahran in March of 1997. But first he had to get there. With all of the charges he faced, flying was a much more dangerous proposition than traveling over land.

To make matters infinitely more difficult, the Saudi government had a policy that all visas had to be issued in a visitor's country of origin. This meant that Swango would have to go back to the United States and risk capture just to get his Saudi visa. Swango argued that it was ridiculous for him to fly all the way to the U.S. and then fly all the way back when South Africa was so much closer to Saudi Arabia. But the Saudi consulate refused to budge.

Was Michael Swango desperate, or just completely insane? Did he not realize that he would be captured upon setting foot in the United States? It's hard to know for sure what was going through his mind. Perhaps his back was against the wall with nowhere else to go, and he thought that just maybe he might get lucky. It was a gamble, it was a roll of the dice, and he went ahead and played the hand he'd been dealt, hoping that he would win big. But on June 27, 1997, as soon as Swango stepped off his plane at O'Hare International Airport in Chicago, he was detained by immigration officials and his passport was confiscated.

As soon as Swango was in custody, he caved. Threatened with extradition back to Zimbabwe, he agreed to plead guilty to the forgery charges that had long ago been leveled against him. Swango put in a guilty plea on a charge of defrauding the government in March of 1998. Just a few months later, in July, he was found guilty and sentenced to three-and-a-half years in prison. But if Swango breathed a sigh of relief while he filled up on prison food and got caught up on the latest American soap operas, expecting to be released in just a few years' time, he was sadly mistaken.

Because while Swango was safely locked away, investigators were compiling enough evidence to put him away for a very long time for all of the other accusations against him. Documents were uncovered and bodies were dug up. After examining medical charts and chemical traces from deceased patients, authorities could prove that Swango had deliberately given his patients lethal doses of medication—and in some cases outright poison.

As a result of this mountain of accumulated evidence, on July 11, 2000, just as Swango was on the verge of finishing his three-and-a-half-year sentence for fraud, he was slapped with three counts of murder and several other lesser charges. He was indicted of all these new charges on July 17. At first, Swango followed the same course of action he had when he was charged with poisoning his coworkers in the 1980s: He pled Not Guilty.

But then prosecutors informed him of the stakes. Should the courts come back with guilty verdicts—and even Swango had to admit that the odds were leaning in that direction—he stood a good chance of getting a death sentence in New York and an even better one of being extradited back to Zimbabwe. It's unclear what Swango feared more—dying, or being extradited and imprisoned in a foreign country that had developed a virulent hatred for him—but he cracked under the pressure once again and agreed to plead guilty.

After everything was said and done, Swango was handed three life terms for the three charges of murder. Now in his late 60s, Swango is still locked away in a maximum-security prison in Florence, Colorado. Since his incarceration in 2000, the previously outspoken Swango has made a point of being silent, refusing all requests for interviews or any other inquiry into his life behind bars.

Does Michael Swango Have Any Remorse?

Even though he pled guilty to his crimes—or at least the crimes that resulted in indictments—in the world of Michael Swango this is a mere technicality in the chess game that he has always played with the world. Even though he entered a guilty plea, his victims will most likely never get a heartfelt confession of guilt from him. Swango continues to present himself as a victim of unjust persecution, and seems determined to continue doing so until the day he dies. It's hard for the rest of the world to understand the darkness that resides in the heart of someone like Swango. We can only hope that there aren't too many more of his disposition out there seeking residencies and doing round-the-clock rotations at our clinics and hospitals.

Further Reading and Resources

Here in this final section, I just wanted to share with you some of the great resources that I made use of in my research for this book.

Angels of Death. Emily Webb
This is a fascinating book that deals specifically with doctors who turn to murder. It is as eye opening as it is frightening. Just be warned—after reading it, you just might reconsider that appointment with the general practitioner!

Serial Killer Files. Harald Schechter
This book is the ultimate resource which lists just about every mass murder and serial killer case known to man. It's not recommended for the faint of heart, but if you are doing research for an academic paper or want to examine a very specific case, this book is for you.

Blind Eye. James Stewart
This book is one of the most in-depth on the subject of Swango, dealing with his childhood to just before his conviction in 2000. The book was written in 1999, so it doesn't quite tell the whole story, but it certainly tells a good nine tenths of it.

New York Times
The *New York Times* has archived all of its old articles and posted them online, which is a great resource if you're doing pre-internet-era research. You can peruse a dispatch dated January 1, 1979, right on your phone. Go to www.newyorktimes.com to find out for yourself.

YouTube
YouTube has a wealth of material on Michael Swango, from the *Justice Files* episode that led to his dismissal in South Dakota to 1980s prison interviews with *20/20*'s John Stossel. Just browse through www.youtube.com for yourself and you will find plenty of archived footage of Dr. Double-O Swango.

Also by Jack Smith

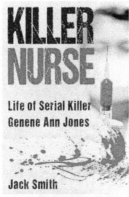

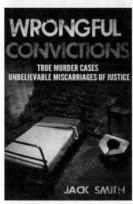

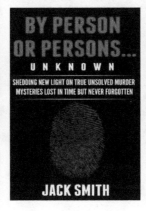

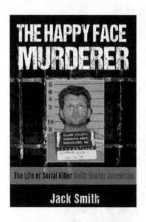

THE HAPPY FACE MURDERER

The Life of Serial Killer Keith Hunter Jesperson

Jack Smith

THE HORRIFIC CRIMES GILLES DE RAIS REVISITED

Life of a Serial Killer of the Middle Ages

Jack Smith

THE BEAST OF BIRKENSHAW

LIFE OF SERIAL KILLER PETER MANUEL

JACK SMITH

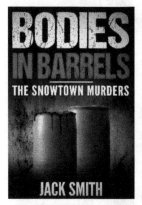

BODIES IN BARRELS

THE SNOWTOWN MURDERS

JACK SMITH

HIDDEN BRUTALITY

LIFE OF SERIAL KILLER CARL EUGENE WATTS

JACK SMITH

THE SPOKANE KILLER

The Life of Serial Killer Robert Lee Yates Jr.

Jack Smith

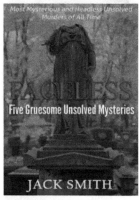

Most Mysterious and Headless Unsolved Murders of All Time

FACELESS

Five Gruesome Unsolved Mysteries

JACK SMITH

The Barton MURDER

The Mysterious and True Murder Story on Hamilton Mountain. Did Someone Get Away With Murder?

Jack Smith

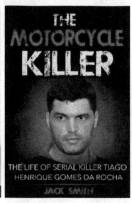

THE MOTORCYCLE KILLER

THE LIFE OF SERIAL KILLER TIAGO HENRIQUE GOMES DA ROCHA

JACK SMITH

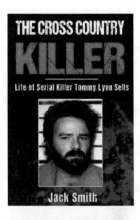

THE CROSS COUNTRY **KILLER**

Life of Serial Killer Tommy Lynn Sells

Jack Smith

ANGEL OF DEATH

Life of Serial Killer Tommy Lynn Sells

Jack Smith

TRUE CRIME STORIES OF CLAIRVOYANTS SOLVING MURDER CASES

REAL LIFE PSYCHIC DETECTIVES

JACK SMITH

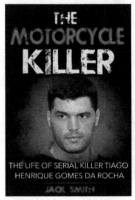

THE MOTORCYCLE **KILLER**

THE LIFE OF SERIAL KILLER TIAGO HENRIQUE GOMES DA ROCHA

JACK SMITH

THE MOST DEVIOUS KILLERS OF ALL TIME

Crafty Serial Killers who Objectified their Victims for their Own Twisted Needs

Jack Smith

THE BUTCHER **BAKER**

Life of Serial Killer Robert Christian Hansen

Jack Smith

CPSIA information can be obtained
at www.ICGtesting.com
Printed in the USA
LVHW011917220821
695831LV00018B/2075

9 781983 684753